A DORLING KINDERSLEY BOOK

Note to parents

My New Puppy is designed to help the very young develop a sense of responsibility toward a new pet and encourages greater awareness of a puppy's needs. Each scene introduces a new experience and one aspect of petcare. By looking at this photographic story together and using each page as a starting point for discussion, you will help your child understand that caring for a pet is sometimes challenging but can be a rewarding experience, too!

Editor Sheila Hanly
Art Editor Nicki Simmonds
U.S. Editor B. Alison Weir
Senior Art Editor Mark Richards
Production Controller Marguerite Fenn
Managing Editor Jane Yorke
Art Director Roger Priddy

Photography by Steve Shott
Illustrations by Conny Jude
Model Jack Richards
Puppies supplied by Intellectual Animals

First American Edition, 1992
10 9 8 7 6 5 4 3 2 1

Dorling Kindersley Inc., 232 Madison Avenue, New York, New York 10016

Copyright © 1992 Dorling Kindersley Limited, London

ISBN: 1-879431-77-7

Library of Congress Catalog Card Number : 91-58200

Color reproduction by Colourscan
Printed in Italy by New Interlitho

STARTING
OUT

My New Puppy

Written by Harriet Hains

DORLING KINDERSLEY, INC.

NEW YORK

Making friends

Jack has a new puppy. Her name is Honey.
"Here's a ball to play with, Honey," says Jack.

Honey chases the ball.
She rolls it with her paw.
Jack gives Honey lots
of other toys too.
They have fun together,
and soon they are
the best of friends.

Time for a walk

"Let's go for a walk,
Honey," calls Jack.
He puts on his coat
and boots.
Honey wags her tail.
She likes walks.

"You have to wear your
collar and leash outside,"
Jack tells the puppy.
He puts on his backpack.
Now they are both ready to go.

Off to the park

It's a sunny day, so Jack
takes Honey to the park.
Honey tugs on her leash.
There's lots to see –
and a cat to chase!
Jack holds on tightly
to Honey's leash.

Fun and games

Once they reach the
park, Jack lets the
puppy off her leash.
"Look, Honey, fetch!"
calls Jack.
He throws a stick
for her to chase.

Honey runs after the stick. "Hey, you're supposed to bring it back," says Jack.

But Honey wants to chew the stick instead.

Heading home

It's time to go home.
"Come on, Honey,"
says Jack.
But Honey wants
to stay and play.
She likes it in the park.

It starts to rain. Jack puts up his umbrella.
Honey decides to go home after all.

Keeping clean

Now they are home and out of the rain. Jack takes off his wet coat and boots. Honey's paws are wet too. She leaves muddy paw prints all over the floor.

"I'd better get you clean
and dry," says Jack.
He rubs Honey's fur
with a towel.
Then he brushes her all over.
Honey likes being brushed.

Dinnertime

The puppy is hungry and thirsty after her walk. Jack gives her a bowl of fresh water to drink.

"Now, how about something to eat?"
Jack gives Honey her favorite dog biscuits.
She eats them all up, lickety-split!

Time for a rest

Honey feels very sleepy. It's time for a nap.
She climbs into her basket and snuggles down.

Jack quietly leaves
his sleeping puppy.
He plays with his
toy dog instead.
"It's nice to have a new
friend," thinks Jack.
"But I won't forget
my old friends
either!"

5

E
MARTIN, Ann M.
Leo the Magnificat